Hot Sun,
Cold Water

Acknowledgments

Executive Editor: Diane Sharpe

Supervising Editor: Stephanie Muller

Design Manager: Sharon Golden

Page Design: Simon Balley Design Associates

Photography: Bruce Coleman: cover (bottom left), (John Shaw) page 21; Greg Evans: page 11; Robert Harding: page 20, 25; Tony Stone: cover (top right, middle right), pages 19, 22, 23, 24, 26; ZEFA: cover (middle left), pages 9, 18.

ISBN 0-8114-3703-5

1 2 3 4 5 6 7 8 9 0 PO 00 99 98 97 96 95 94

Hot
Sun,
Cold
Water

Paul Humphrey

Illustrated by

Sarah Young

STECK-VAUGHN
C O M P A N Y
ELEMENTARY · SECONDARY · ADULT · LIBRARY

4

7

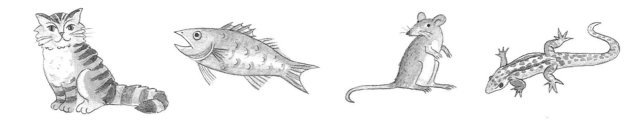

8

But this water is cold.

The rocks get hot in the sun.

10

But it is still cool in the tide pool.

12

13

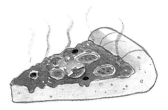

My French fries are hot.

14

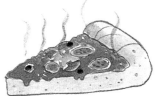

My ice cream is cold.

15

16

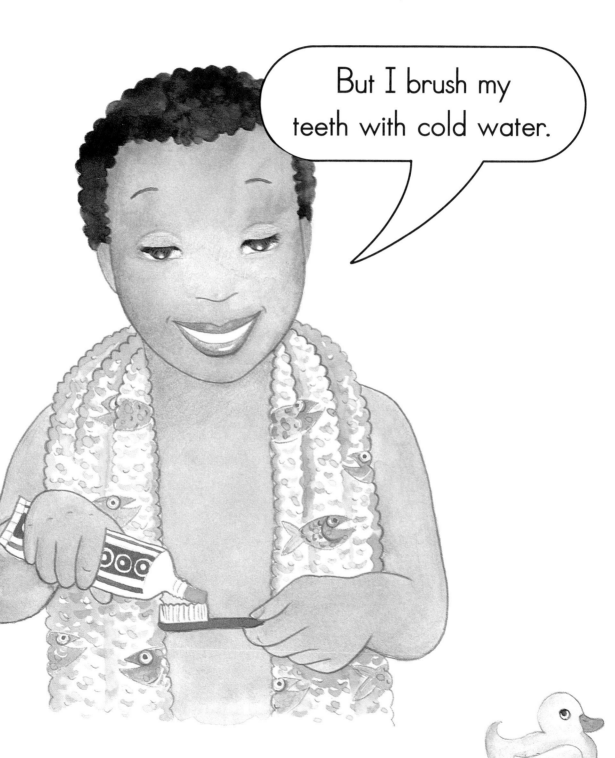

But I brush my teeth with cold water.

It is hot in the desert.

18

But it is cold at the North Pole.

19

It is hot in the rain forest.

But it is cold on top of the mountain.

Crocodiles live where it is hot.

22

Penguins live where it is cold.

23

Some people live where it is hot.

Some people live where it is cold.

It may be hot during the day.

But it is cooler at night.

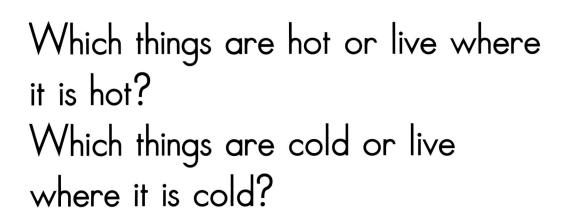

Which things are hot or live where it is hot?

Which things are cold or live where it is cold?

30

Index